by Isabel Thomas
illustrated by Richard Watson

What happens to rubbish?

Rubbish might get into a river.
It might harm animals.

How can I cut down my rubbish?

You might put things in the bin.

Stop!

You can fix this.

How can I fix a zip?

Rub the soap along the zip.
Now you can pull the zip!

How can I fix a chip?

Rub wax on the chip.
It will fill the chip.

How can I fix a mark?

Soak the mark with lemon.
The mark will vanish!

How can I fix worn things?

1. Put a mark high up.

2. Cut along the mark.

3. Turn them into shorts!

What if I can not fix it?

You can turn it into lots of things!

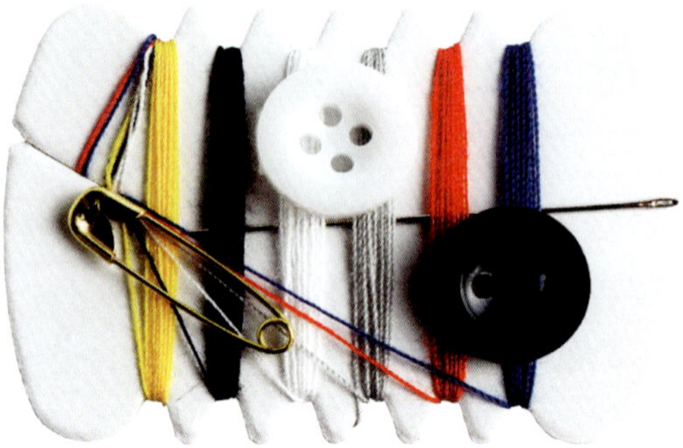

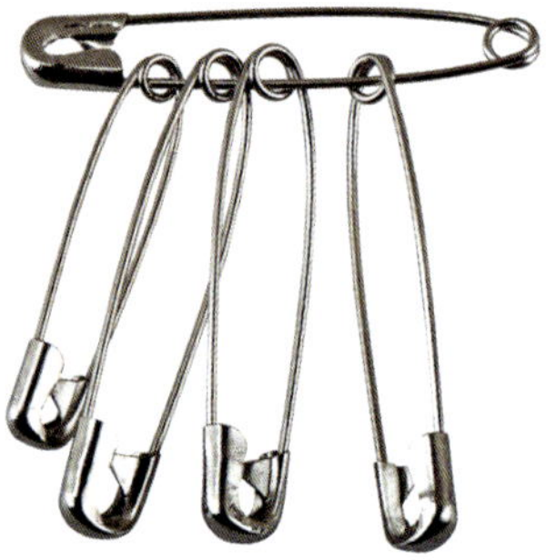

Encourage students to say how to fix things, using the pictures.